Pale Wester

Issued by Lazy R Softcovers.
Lazy Cloud Estates, *Turnagain By the Sea*,
Western Hesperides, Arctican-Boreal Republic

Fourth Edition Theta Mu-7
November, 2023
(First published in 2019)

The portrait appending the Overture (Novalis, German Romantic Philosopher/Poet) is from Wikipedia. Credit Neko for title page photo.

Cover art: *The Return*, Thomas Cole, 1837
Copyright© 02023 All rights reserved worldwide.

Infinite radiance...
Divine uniquity
Reflecting the eternal Life
Of all lovely things...

Pale Western Star:
The Poetry of Robin Devoe

*They ne'er betide set,
in spring, nor winter
to slumber, nor sweeten more,
than leafy hills of sundown glinter...*

– Robin Devoe, *Lost Tuvan Princess*

Table of Contents

Overture ...	1
I. The Season of Light	8
II. Hazel Luminescence	15
III. Poetical Mindswirl	21
IV. In Morpheus	34
V. Sweet Melange	41
VI. Passages Parallel	46
VII. Pale Western Star	52
VIII. Seven Hills Ski Park Chart	85
IX. The Neverlands	86
X. Lost Tuvan Princess	88
Quotations	104
...The Last Page	106

Overture ...

Is there a poetry of light and sky that celebrates beauty, ecstasy... the sublime hope to explore Nature's distant desiderata, Her far, beckoning aspect, Her love for humankind, Her soul's aspiration? Here wouldst lie the horizon dream from which hearts attune may feel a renascent Truth infusing their most sacred strains of thought.

Modes of versification evolve through the transforming sensibility of spiritualizing souls. Spontaneous outflows reflected upon, Poesy's aerial dreams pondered – these repeatedly recast from higher and higher views may coax open the petals of flowerings both profound in Beauty, purified in Truth...

Ten chapter descriptions follow (poem titles are in bold):

I. The Season of Light

Conceived whilst riding that wild current of twilight boldly coursing thru deep, cerulean nights – that summer light, that luminous gloam, seeming bred especial for the boreal lands where Nature unveils Her soul most beautiful, Her countenance most sacred. Cycling the fringe of that land's blue dream, the eternal city slept, while at half past two morning bells, riders alone feel the mysterious, powerful love of the western horizon's twitterlight as a soft presence most palpable. That horizon light was proof of the Divine, Her window toward the limit of what mortals may perceive of perfection. Eyes upon that horizon for seemingly endless, pure, blazing moments filled with an intense, glorious rapture beyond understanding – these secret times, the most sacred and joyous of an Age, soul buoyed toward what strange and lovely heights?

May we call this most exquisite twilight, tinging the sky deep within the boreal half-night, and all the sweet feelings that constellate around it (including, it seems, some of the strongest and noblest feelings of which humans are capable) – Yes we name this divine hint of heaven *the Fleeting Azurine*. It's a permeating coda in such poems as **Twilight**, **Heaven's Faintest Star**, **luniversal lispers**, and **Horizon Dream**. **Past Her Purple Hills** may offer the purest illustration of this theme: sunset, the horizon, the sky's tincture – painted with a tenderness of feeling, with a sweet vibrant tone of an emotion approaching the divine.

Sensitive to this spiritualising force in nature, one must yet fight against this sensitivity's tendency to diminish with age, as the world tries to blinker one's spiritual sight:

Yon Crescent Moon, as fixed as if it grew
In its own cloudless, starless lake of blue;
I see them all so excellently fair,
I see, not feel, how beautiful they are!"
– Samuel Taylor Coleridge, *Dejection: an Ode*

II. Hazel Luminescence

A quality found in human love, close allied to the Fleeting Azurine, we term *Hazel Luminescence* – sometimes the flush of romantic first blush is cast from within one's own soul, through eyes green or brown, onto the adored, and reflected back through the many filters on the perception of mortal beauty. Within the eyes of our beloved, we see the hazel eyes of our animae, avatars of inmost life and dreams, beaming back. Within this poetical grouping **Shimmering Center** shows well – a sprinkling of quotations (Shelley, Tennyson, Keats) neatly lace together an essential expression of the *Hazel Luminescence*. The italicized passage in **Bound By Ancient Longing** is within this volume the loveliest, perhaps.

III. Poetical Mindswirl

Most beauty-filled – these vague, dreamlike, lisping works: *the Poetical Mindswirl*. Genesized after exposure to Carroll's *Jabberwocky* and

Joyce's *Finnegan's Wake,* within this style we strain to see the trellis-work supporting those "dreaming spires," most delicate and beautiful – and just as we think a tiny sphere of infinite beauty pinnacles atop some sublime steeple, one blink brings her tumbling down from heaven. Some tumble gloriously: *subtle intimations of ideal beauty lingering aloft the wreckage.*

Pristina Aventis sets a transmaterial romantic scene of seemingly impossible beauty. **Yester's Mysterium** dives into a proesy of flowing meter whilst weaving phantastical words around arcane, lovingly-purpled feelings – sense conveyed more through sound, rhythm, rhyme and association, perhaps searching (tho in vain) for a primeval language operating on a deeper, less rational level than that of our everyday speech. **The Azurine Bellerium** adumbrates yet another twitterlight dream, while **In Cirrus Wisp Woven** strives to cast an image of "far-shimmering" divinities.

IV. In Morpheus

The themes in this chapter cluster around a sense of dream or sleep. **Glistering From Her Womb**, **Oneiromantic Mourning**, and **Dare Tease Hypnos** began as one poem that grew unwieldy enough to be cleaved in thirds. **The**

Dreaming Spire – a prose-poem, *à la mode de* Baudelaire – is the only work sprung directly from an actual sleeping dream.

V. Sweet Melange
Verse not fitting elsewhere lay here: one stanza beauties; classically-framed pieces; and epistolary poems. Spanning mere seconds of arc along the spectrum of poetical craft, some single stanza poems do seem incommensurately illumined. **Avatars of Gold** is one such meteor, flashing portentous meaning, perhaps, across the star-filled firmament. The ponderous meter of **Enlightened Beauty** serves well the theme. **Deeping Legends of a Purple Land** could be considered narrative verse, though it is not a long piece and waxes lyrical.

VI. Passages Parallel
Paired poems: the first employs extremely obscure (though at times quite beautiful) language; the second translates the first passage into our common English tongue. **Dynasties of Artistic Woodland** plays near the height of this fancy.

VII. Pale Western Star
This versified tale explores themes of romance, death, and illusion whilst interlarding not a few

lavish & lyric passages – orchids upon the moor:
> Love entire bound within the stroke
> Of lightning upon the midnight oak.

VIII. Seven Hills Ski Park Chart attends the Neverlands poem and combines geographic truth with literary fancy, whilst imaging ideal visions of a seemingly attainable paradise.

IX. The Neverlands
These lands (also known as Seven Hills Ski Park) did profoundly impact the waking and dream life of a poetical youth; and did host many bliss-filled hours, this obscure, lovely swatch of wood (birch and spruce) half an hour's cycle from the Lazy Cloud Estate. Thru the citizen forester's own ministrations, faint moose paths blossomed into an intimate latticework of trails, upon which to ski, frolic, and canter. The poem is a dream of what she might become, these 200 acres of hill, meadow, wood, and vale interlaced with narrow paths where those most attune with the subtle aesthetic may roam, sport, and spiritually grow.

X. Lost Tuvan Princess
This dramatic verse traces the desperate flight of a Tuvan royal, separated from her tribe, harboring a complex history, and displaying daring strength & grace of ski and pole. She

flees from Boreal Turkmen assassins across the white crystal of sun-slanting snowscapes.

Robin Devoe
Summer Solstice, 02023
Lazy Cloud Estates, Western Hesperides

I. The Season of Light

Heaven's Faintest Star
The horizon mother seems so far
to stretch beyond our dreaming grasp;
So far, far She seems, yet such beauty lies
enrapturing her extremes, we sense Her feel
from a molten heart, ancient as the hills,
the soft voice of pure feeling speaks,
to unwind the shroud of mortal wills
that cloaks a light divine.

And there She lingers, our *Fleeting Azurine*
upon the horizon's far, feeling sea;
Awakening the still, spiritual dream
beyond Heaven's faintest star.

Horizon Dream
Lost horizons within, the mystery
a far-cast eye informs:
Impressions still of hope and dream;
Shimmering distant within the deep
fallen fringe of rainbow hues, nesting –
but an hour's run past far, sloping lands:
Where eviternity may all life enrapture.

luniversal lispers
The twilight's deepening still –
deepening... deepening almost until
without ears that hear, nor eyes for sight
faintly, that distant land you *feel:*
The world we know is disappearing,
as soft whispers beckon
from within horizon light.

Luniversal still, lispers echo –
these *feeling liturgies*,
rising beyond the shore
piping tones from these –
our *sunken* gods no more.

Mortal Lamentations
The soft-pillowed cloud
staged in twilight, gleaming;
The stars of summer, clinging
still to sky, pale above the sea,
the peaks, past hills mantled in oak:
the whole beautiful savage crown
of this mortal dream – everything:
less real than shadows seem.

Banquet of distant skies! Unroll the glory
Within these haunts of rising tone
To softly murmur the heart along
This thrill frisson of ecstacies sublime.

Yet Why within feelings divine
Do mortal parts still weep wine?
May such Beauty
never in life be true?

Votive Light
There lies a wondrous light
fading distant across our sky;
Above the western rise, a glimmer,
o'er the faint purpureal peak,
and green-robed hill –
Softly, these marvelled hues,
these numberless boreal midnights,
of spiritual youth may sing.

A hint of fancied things,
lingering just past the last horizon shade
and stretched beyond the beautiful:
A perfect universe, it seems –
the quiet, rapturous ponderings
of what diviner numenal thought?

And as this glimmering beauty
holds the world in quiet rapture
we spy a deeper light that seems to shine
from the very eye of God...
in transcendent wishes for future glory
we feel there is no pain – no past nor present
in the wide, wide universe
Beauty... is All –

pervading every soul-filled dream.
And midst this feeling wave's undulant ravish
riding the warm, tremulous swell,
we see the crest and almost choose
sacrifice to this great Muse –
For by such feeling could we live
to taste what eternity alone may give:
the shim'ring fruit of Paradise?

Past Her Purple Hills

The far-sloped lands seem to feed,
the distant skies pervade,
in numinous tones the horizon speaks
and paints the twilit steeps
in hues of hope for humankind.

The faint stars of half-night fade
past Her purple western hills,
whose gleam will never yield
beauty, nor love, nor truth
to worlds of darkening shade.

The Skies Dreaming

Upon horizon hues, to gaze
(Trailing above a sunken sun's dream)
Wondering in ten-thousand colored ways:
"What's this Fleeting Azurine?

Yes... what is this feeling –
This Fleeting Azurine?
Issuing from the vesperal berth
Of all we wish for life, all we wish for Earth?

What's this feeling
That lends to love immortal tasting?
How so sensuous, yet so chasting?
Where floats this waking dream?"

Tis Truth & Glory that beckons you
From your mad mortal seem –
Tis Love that leads to you
Your divine and grandest clue:
This, your Fleeting Azurine.

"Yes I have seen that subtle gleam
(the faint blue shimmer above far trees)
In answer to mortaling, midnight pleas?
The only truth in life's cold dream?"

See through our mystery-woven seam
Into our Love's soul-thing –
See past your mortal waking dream
Feel part of the Whole being.

"I shall!... I shall, yet wait whole One,
Wait on me to unveil your gleam
To feel your bright, undying beam –
To win the Heaven we have won!"

Know not wait – tis only Now...
If one could but see past fear,
You would awake this now to Here –
Just watch, feel... and pray,
(eyes on this horizon mirror)
Reflecting our love until the day
Earth's every tear dissolves away.

The Sunset
Watch the Sun out-set far hills
The glory of the human race run
Thru a fiery grave plumb:
Til, in molten shivers, She pause to rave
And there to roil in highest beauty,
Until the last lavender shade
Into Her collecting dark does fade.

Twilight
Summer twilight oft may seem
Like a wild sun's last glimmering
From far beyond the ranging hills –
A mystic, burning glory cast
Upon our horizon's distant dream:
With ideal Souls aborning...

Diviner Edge

To pause mid life's sweeter part
and see the dying of the day –
a late child of lingering Spring,
forged within no edge diviner
the horizon dreams of Nature's fire;
Upon a moment's crest, slow-weaned
there, in high loveliness, weltering...
To finally burst forth its lifeful ravish
of Truth... and Love... and Youth –
and then begin the slow dark fade
beneath a purple-feathered sky...

II. **Hazel Luminescence**

Upon Gloaming Shore
Cycling late, smokefall
Clustering the coast –
In the golden blink of sun-doven summers
we pass near.

A classic face, beaming
Such joy and hope for life;
Laughter
And loveliness sweet intermingling...
God-sprung, the spirit seeming
Ancient, yet cast from thoughts still green.

The gloaming embodiment
Of most beautiful truth
Suckling pure, spiritual milk
from the delicate and delicious light –
Together, we ride
along the blue fade
of what lovelier boreal midnight shore?

Bound by Ancient Longing
Bound by ancient longing,
by the hope of eternal belonging;
One waits upon that golden she,
dreaming her to come
(past horizons unwon);
til her gilt countenance, at last may seem
to meet that self-cast dream.

And so we touch, speaking pleasures
upon the midnight moan
sinking the measure of our souls;
But young were we, soon falling
toward "love's sad satieties" –
Too full of love, we loved it seems
falsely imaged destinies.

The heart by deepest sorrows chilled, (the shiver
in which the soul itself seems to quiver)
thinking what was so late, so sweet –
So sweet this mourning-cloak of loneness cast
upon those thoughts that dared to sing...
yet, melancholic the wake of this that passed
wrapped in feelings of numinous dream.

Shimmering Center
Creative feelings breathe in...
creative feelings
      breathe out
like zephyrs on flowering hills,
you inspire orchids promethean,
      & roses amaranthine –
deeply, life you vivify:
enticing one to be
      more sublime in quest,
more sensitive in perception.

Shelleyan lines climb to mind:
"none ever trembled and panted with bliss
in the garden, the field, or the wilderness" –
none like a softly striving soul
quivering beneath unique expression.

These creative feelings breathe
into this shimmering center –
      You breathe
into this shimmering center;
till within your eyes and through
a world's aurorean wonder I see:
"beyond the sunset and the baths
      of all the western stars"
above the ocean's far horizon seams
"huge cloudy symbols of a high romance"
intimate our future – mystic & unwritten,
like the distant summer night

when such spirit the other finds
      beneath an ethereal moon.
These spirits... so deeply a'quiver;
til the purpureal plant of noble desire
unleash its rhythmic pulse
      echoing from tendrils of unseen power –
Vibrant power!
      – Lightning from the ocean's floor sprung.

Soul Echo
From nowhere came the fated she
to stir the thought: "I think,
she the love, she the link,
to interfuse dreams of destiny."

Her soul-life weaved throughout from whence
these thoughts and feelings came alone,
as if she spoke for all life hence,
as if whole, complete were the taste –
what sweet issuance, without haste,
wouldst emerge, gestated with all desire –
      with the rare, effluvial fire,
of love, burning for birth
to spill o'er the weeping Earth.

Yet she caught the dance
thru halls self-hallowed
thru the vacant castle of ethered joy –
the floating horizons of youth
where in vain we search for love... and for truth

where wallowed within one's own Bellerium
in seeming we love, and laugh
at twisting fancy, at mere delirium –
at meaninglessness, wafting and wisping.

And then to wake in pain of thought,
and see the glimmer where she passed;
And know this love as forged from naught,
but that which does not ever last.

To Athena
An isle lone mid endless blue
    Shaded by zephyrus clouds o'er sailing
The immortal sand and passing dew:
    Reason fly! the moon's a'paling
    Above Athena, grey and wailing
Over logic lost in beauty's hue.

May knowledge cold cease to loom
Above, cease casting gloom
Cease forcing death before we bloom.

Let Romantic visions reign!
The hope to breathe an eternal wish
To know the inmost glory and bliss:
If this ideal be unforsaken
No worldly force may ever break in.

Mingling Divinities
Here we find communion
to sing with soft, poetic sighs;
to breathe together beyond the rise
of past divinities mingled
those raw joys, cascading
through each soul's affinities singled.

Spiritual awareness slowly dawns
as the universe wells up within;
and finally we know
the vivified touch of another.

Lifefulness So Soon
What lifefulness so soon –
from whence... and how to whom?

Such deep feelings rose
into a life whose only heat
lay deep within the coals:
an ocean's beauty
clustering sequestered shoals...

And now the inspiration
of these unexpected hours:
sunshine from beneath the sea –
uncurling inner flowers.

III. Poetical Mindswirl

Yesters Mysterium

I

We conjure the land's deep shimmer
Within the mindcrack, subtle the glimmer –
& all wishes extend beyond me:
Blooming through dark-petaled ever-night...

Phantasies interpenetrate
Our collective belief: such madness
Seems to shape the world,
Seems to cloister us in sadness;
And though we bound nor tethered be
This rough wave of thought, this mortal cumulus
Raves across their skies own universe –
A luniverse, really, twisting reality's edge
And sealing the undivided fate
Of espied horizons from imaginings preaureate.

II

How to truly gather and balance all that must be,
    And yet not let
        Sloth or squantering ever inserpentine?
We pretend to tease that noble Jester
Of phylus life –
Captain of our sundered fleet which,
    mastered or served,

Knows where within we sink.
Volition alone canst sever the head
from the beast who's twining insidious inside.
So what can be done? We can't seam to sow
What reapeth not,
neither can we uncloak ourselves
      without the Innerseeming;

What's even verse, we do not grok
the working essence
Of soul-merging communions.
No, we glean not even a rosary
      From votive pluckings of proesy,
Lest we sempiternally sacrifice all for Truth.
In veritas we the pressed masses
are philous and tangent to such primal stirrings,
But we can't ever quite brush aside
whatever roils like four reels of madness
strung past this conscious grasping of ours.
The seconds slip ungrippable:
That's the quenching wave
of reality's only fealty –
      (we believe it could be
      what we can't quite see:
a rorid Microcosm
Mirroring the years of tears
upon a mourning leaf) –
Nature sends herself breaming back to us...
and that's why one can't quite escape,

Why all that's happening is within reach
(if not in view);
     Why all the gloaming Janes
     reflect your animas' second hue –
& all the Daemons are shriking
     From within our own skull-gated zoo.

This whole weirder luniverse,
a mindwave just cresting
From what within you is already jesting –
It's madness, we glow...
     With Promethean fires to forge
Worldspines to plumb these bottomless times...

          III
My latent hopes spew forth as lava
     Into the Maelstrom's oceanic door,
     This great sorrow's motionless core,
The Whirled is spiraling netherous toward.
We hear the inner chiming of what mad father
Peeling His ticks and dismoored tocks
Across the lochs of Yester's Mysterium?

     And still the ship won't sail
Toward my distant peak's imagining –
It's like life sunk past
what my feet couldn't keep under¡

IV
What sounds from Soul's own ocean?
    Where tears the primal Eye?
What waves of sweet emotion,
    Lap beyond the Western sky?
The truth in whispered tiding
May ebb and flood inside us,
    The Sun's gleaming,
The seas deep moon-beaming –
    The One within the inner seeming
Of such madding mystery –
Inspires still the life
    That stirs a soul to song –
    To strive, to search... to long
For the mystic tones
piping the heart's fullest expression...

The Dews Onfire, Queen Worldgreen
Queen Worldgreen, the dews onfire!
and Gaea yields to a darker power –
the once perslucent cumuli
lie darkling as the last true lumens die...

With tainted souls the Earth's awash
in streaming shame, her face is
the lachrymide wasting
of all human races.

She fever-flashes in smoldered blinking:
"Cannot the sacred orbs unquoth their nebereth?

The spueres of whole light
Finally realize their higher sentient?
Cannot the flausted heroes
Leastly cire the Maddening?
Or dirge shanklings profound with seeming
Upon those shores of endless dreaming?"

No, rapt in desperate waverings
unable to worship the distant light
(our souls – voiceless, quavering)
shy behind the numens of night;

Unreflective, we cling to fears,
opening the mind to joy, nor tears –
nor to dirge, nor to sing
nor profound with seeming
to wander those shores of endless dreaming...

Queen Worldgreen, across the ocean
the dews on fire, the dews on fire!
And the dream of what sweet emotion
spouts from what shimmering spire?
And Greenworld visions seem to cry
From what sensitive stretch of sky?

...and still upward and on an outrisen moon
shimbles toward Nadaria.

WelkinBlue Weeping

A scagdrills current o'er-sweeps our Gestrus,
as the mad mass shrikes – craven, scattered –
Skullshires clump as the third hour strikes
cloistering all that was pregnant with goodness.

Science, we think, has fully fathomed
life's infinite Waters, our mystic bathos;
the seemingly sated daily thirsts –
but He feeds not the soul
nor answers the faint, spiritual cry.

Yet, more attune sound the pipings
of Gaia's choral depths, inaureate – so below
as above, the Welkens cerulean ride
on vaulted domes of primatrice sunglide;
And the virga still steams,
and alborado, sky-bourne dreams,
Lift the nester avis unto higher cirrus,
as the vespertine Prophet sleeks beyond
the last ridges' deatheraging burnbright –
So to countenance the beauty
of lachrymide humanity's last gloaming duty.

Even as great WelkinBlue's weeping,
beneath another sky, shriven
(another azure summer seeping),
another phantasy, sun-scorched and riven.

Thousand Year Numen
The skyrising aerilot's
luvenescent revolution
is within itself written –
The seamed vestures of such hope
feed & clothe all primal stimulus.

Aethered and tithering, Youth
passionate still these whirling thoughts
canst uncover a soul's poise;
The id hunkers, festrish within, and crescing
destined to explode in one parsed blink –,
or sourly seep
thru a taosand years susurration.

The sleathings quail, thinking no unthought
mesmers to surpast the dawn
as quiet blades of hopeless soar,
wailing for the next heart to splunge –
unless answers we find to slaken
those questings once shunned...

The Azurine Bellerium
Far above the sunset line
I gaze into Her life with mine:
souls wrapped within the streams
of emotions flowing from common dreams.

The caperous maddening gambols along
riding abreast luniversal thought

we think the universe our everaster:
we dream...and think we see past Her.

No subtler urge reloosed upon we –
(darst unheed?)
To plant full-slurch a cusp on Her nymphlium
to dapple and dip in limnus cumulids...
all languille and tremulous in undulant insania?
No matter the haste,
we'd sapphire each trillium...
Such words seem to spell
a furious squalm unspirituelle
leading the eyes of gods astray
as hearts gorge toward seeming bliss.

And we, the shadow dreams
spew charm; spew song,
yet sing a less charming end e'er long:
as we overquaff the azurine etherium
and swallowing hearts, ride for Bellerium.

Now far above the sunset line
Her soul commingles its life with mine
as in horizon glow we gleam;
and deeply drink the azurine,
interpenetrating the one great dream
a wisping lip only half remesmers:
Still trusting that still, strange power
constellating all we ever knew.

Renascent Apocrapha
Things are knotted as they seam
when we fell out of dream:
unspinning the Whirled Tapestry,
Her threads of silver light
Her night asters hissing into ocean,
as the world's cloistered emotion
unfurls expressions of Spirit –
fashioned for those that'd hear it.

Lurking Hour
These days crawl by
linking hours with unthinklings dour
while the craven quail their hearts from
underskirt...

When will these counter-cocked prinkers
      unpride their dondlings?
And wherefore doze these dramskulls
wheedling dreads we don't sever needs?

Numens formicate beneath Albasian mid-nights
(surpasting all hope), while driven leavings
seemlessly wander this now ridden quease –
it's the whole millennium's monomoronic tease!

We feel so -escent with yester eve's questing
yet cannot become
what the mourning foremade us;
And think not upon the sharking hour

of the world's quenchless thirst
for blood and tears too answerless.

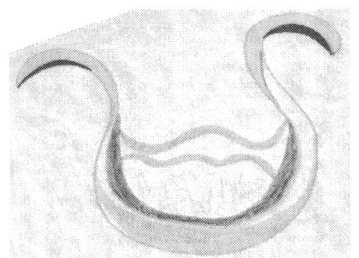

Chimpion's Prate
In heaving chaunt, in whisper
they conjure worlds to come;
With fevered heart, the wisher
of things far past undone...

Primal lyres strain
toward a distant heaven's murmuring –
ancient echoes flung past the shimmering
soul-fires asleep beyond the sea.

Evolution's unseen dream shimbles on
not ever quite seeming to pine
the thoughtful tone on a monkey's wail;
nor steal a sprig of manna
from a primative chimpion's prate.

The dervish seconds strike their beat
to the operatic, thrill twirl
of this – hour planned nut's orbituary –

still spinning from the poison
of mankind's collecting spate.

Shrikes and moans will our chorus be;
Echoing threads through the bellicosity
of this age's dying plunge:
"Her tapestries, a century aflame."

And the World Ash canst cast shade,
for every lily Wanderjahring
through a thousand Ages of pathless dreaming,
wending the headless way
from strands of desert to an ocean's slake;
Unsatiating as love to hearts of clay, seeming
like the desert's salt or a sea of sand...
And the rasping tears lap alone
Upon no stranger land.

In Cirrus Wisp Woven
The ten-taosand fancies a'twirling
inside our own mindfulness
canst downdream what's unfoldering
just beyond the grasper mortal.

Horizons, flame far-shimmering,
Liberi at play in divinity
portend eternal Beauty, blazing
across the eastern skies' affinity –
wishes & wisping in cirrus weave.

Know that you're the one unleashing
glories that dream... and burn –
lispen to yon yesteryearn
       & within lost whensday's thunder
       Hark – the peel of waking wonder!

You know what we glean?
Or are we lost in the caper & frolic,
mid the green,
of rhyming meadows of mountaindream?
No, there is somehow a taste
       of universal gladness
       found in these things we spew
       when we're all insane and new;
Now listen klispish –
She's not lude enough to shrike it!

Pristina Aventis
Togather we, beneath crystalline acclivity
Rave into the other, mellifluently bedewed
And pillowed in cumuli;
Quick-rills sing your rhinis trimbles
As Gankerings whimwelp long, soft chindles
And the ming-phyres sink
beyond purpureal twills...

Lark! Ho, the cries of Alatia poetously rise,
Wisping to Luna in half-mad surmise
Of a night passing through chronos pantillate –
The intimate vespers of nectarous busqueda,
Alive, prequacious... yet interminable –
As ever and on endless lovers do dream.

Warm, Promethean Suns
The golden palpus of our Art
transfigures all we touch:
As aestival zephyrs seed
a distant sky's gestivity.

Souls afloat on ether,
sail between the far-flung fires:
Suckling nature's warm,
Promethean suns.

IV. In Morpheus

Where Lavish Rapture Lay
She woke, as we – in thought & feeling
evoked from bodies spent
beyond *where lavish rapture lay*,
(ravished and reeling)
within a land, distant seeming,
where each slight emotion
expands to fill the worldocean:
lapping beneath no dream so sweet.

Glistering From Her Womb
This day beyond we pass in sleep
an age in Morpheus, sunken deep:
These quaking, lovely thoughts
(shivering along the dew
of ancient, dreaming pastures)
roaming for glory, sought in waking
strangely dulled in dawn's approach –
Fringeless sunrise shades of life, adorning
the first collective human mourning.

Then, springing back,
we surge up the worldspine
children of whirling
through mad meadows divine;
Taming the world in feral kisses
thrown from inner wildernesses

where renascent souls spew flame
as from "clouds of glory," she sang:

"I sing, I sing
of the great golden dream
a vision recast by horizons agleam;
Here is beauty, here is fate:
here is the eternal
banishment of hate."

These dreams of glory reeling
within that land's intenser feeling –
What we do not know, we cannot teach:
the force of legend, spoke beyond speech.

These hidden pulses behind our sight
these lifeful seepings of the shade –
(where younger souls may have played)
Beneath His shadow, the sleeping mind's
blind eye first comes to light
upon the sudden end of night,
when we wake, but rise not nor shine;
Our thinking waves still slumbering roll
toward the shore, the last sighing
beyond what seemed but was not death.

Death – the thought a life will quell
before a sleeping universe unweaves Her spell;
and common feeling of conscious breath
beckons the sleeper's soul to birth,

silencing dreams within their tomb –
So only she of enlightened earth
can wake still glistering from Her womb.

Dare Tease Hypnos
Who so pervades this day
(half-dissolved in the current
of these strange seas)
past shimmered tapestries, beaming
awareness of my own inner seeming?

So gently upon the threshold you plunder
(slipping through what purple-hilled wonder)
yet now dare tease Hypnos awake?
Who seemed so somnolent, mesmering
past the pillowed lavender loom
afore the god-cycle thrust,
eyes unshuttering the lumen must
wreak the orchid's nightly bloom;
mid the stirrings of this that wakes...
as thoughts rise, the soul recloaks,
and love softly expires.

Oneiromantic Mourning
What creative lover's transmaterial touch
dares wend its way to Nod?
Who dare distend the deep-dreamt coil?
Whose breath morphs asunder
the pink horizon cloud?

This world, woven within the wonder
of Phantasy eternal seeming –
this world that still, still lies gleaming,
even as its plume doth fade;
And still may soul lie dreaming
within the purpureal shade.

Who so grips the timorous edge
of Dawn – the Aurorean height,
where sleepers stride blind?
Where Morpheus in zephyrus hand
cast the wakers upon Her strand?

Grasp back for what else lay
glittered upon the shore of night –
the wine-dark memories, the fluttering ocean –
Catching breath mid the glimmering sway
to span across the waters
toward half-lit caves where Memory's daughters
languidly splay the foamy edge
that Lethe's ebb doth usher...

Crossing, back to the world we knew
finally disgorged, we rise and chaunt
above distant shores, as if some bright strand
of all we ever hope to understand
flashes forth, candescent, wisping –
daring to teach a brain just lisping
past madness toward a knowing God.

The Dreaming Spire
Spire-side again, and pleasing still, to pause on
the portico and receive the view of stream
through oak-studded sward
sloping toward the green, sun-dazzled sea…

Well-being overflows within. This spire of
triumph! This free, open house of art; this place
of worship; this holy crypt; this travelers' delight;
this finest symbol of all the best in humankind!
What a perfect, lovely place! How fortunate to
return so often!

Crowded the Muzeum is not, though a few
children jounce past, full of glee, knocking from
plinth an Atreus bust (Agamemnon, perhaps) to
shatter and shiver on the marble floor. An
attendant, languid in post-noon warmth, smiles
for their mirth and rises, slow and easily to clear
the fragments.

Wandering amongst the paintings for half a
chime, lost with old masters in worlds more
seemingly real than mine – engaging no one, so
thoroughly rapt mid the ancient pastorals and
archetypal themes. Upon not a few Romantic
landscapes she lingered, to wonder at the palette
such a painter could pull – the perfect sky-borne
hue of dying sun on cirrus wispen; wondering at

the life, hope – at the perfect dreaming rapture this evokes within.

How should one be so sensitive just now to such? Not recently fasting for weeks in a cave, nor fresh off some great poetical triumph, nor devout and meditative in the company of saints. Though idly upon certain eternal thoughts a'ponder, such paltry labors seem unequal to this remunerable bliss.

For some reason the day holds no desire to ascend the 700 (or even hop the lift) to the Spire's Height – aerie most sublime on days such as these. Instead, down to the chapel, more peopled than above: several kneel beneath the icons, while the stain-glassed menagerie hangs subject to some others abstract perusal. Notable is the old mother, standing east of oaken altar: nothing escapes her black vesture, save a holy, agèd visage framed in spare tress, surprisingly dark. Livened, sapphire eyes course the room, watching us all.

Three paces in, the feeling begins: akin to the romantic scenes' evoking, yet more visceral, deep. Transcendent waves of a spiritual, glorious joy bring tears of sweet release – a more perfect feeling there is not. Love, and a peaceful, though potent beauty, seeming let free by a sudden humility. Then a powerful frisson shivered her being – *I am the rod through which divine lightning may course.* At altar, the intensity trebles, then trebles again – till, for several striking seconds, the very foundations, the entire Spire is shaken, vigorously. A few icons crack, shards dropping to the stone paving below.

Then fast fled, though a soul-felt change remains. Standing, shocked though unafraid, the old woman's eyes bore deep. The kneelers arise, and following her stare, divine the agent of this tremulous affinity. Beseeching answers, they approach, awestruck.

"This, no power *from* me, but *thru* – a fulmen, divine and fluent."

Elaborative attempts largely fail.

V. Sweet Melange

Across an Ocean
We leave our love for fancies far,
That seem so sweet in musèd dream –
Like warmth from Heaven's faintest star,
Or Truth in Life's eternal gleam.

We leave her as these thoughts of glory,
Across an ocean hold us, seeming
Rapt within a hero's story
Of ventures fell, of portents dreaming.

So we left our love for fancies far,
That seemed so sweet in musèd dream –
Like warmth from Heaven's faintest star,
Or Truth in Life's eternal gleam.

Enlightened Beauty
Oft have you gazed at lines upon my face
During the passionate time, now lulled in past –
Find beauty not in remembered visage;
But in knowing that tears have traced,
And shall trace their paths until the fast
Of thy absence ends in frenzied kissage.

La Luna Sings to Thee
La Luna sings to thee
Enfolding last night's mystery –
Sings to fill the purple eye,
To wonder, and to wonder why
Until such sight – illumined sleep
Reflects your soul's forgotten deep;
And you wake to walk the wave
Of conscious life beyond the grave.

The Horizon
A purple land beyond the gloaming lies
Hidden, free from mass projection;
Yet visible to hallowed eyes:
And glory reigns across those skies.

Avatars of Gold
Thinking of love beneath the stars
She feels a Heaven touch the earth:
Like twenty thousand golden avatars
Streaming down to a mortal birth.
And deep beneath the virga dawn
Still, her loveliness wanders on…

Lands Beyond
Find love in each flowering word
Sprung from feathered quilling
Lend these life as Shelley, his bird
And beauty in Wordsworth's daffodilling.

Discover within these rough meters
Devotion & depth, tho in distant heart
(That, once running with the lotus-eaters)
Now serves full the rhyming art.
Peer close, and note the stains
From what rolls now down this face
The dew of love's transparent pains
The wilt of feeling's lost embrace.

All this and more you see, yet know
Twill still be true past life's dying glow.

Skies Within
Upon the bridge, mid forest and hill
to sigh, to shiver, to feel a tear:
sweet distillate of hidden being
melting from that inner sky
where an ocean's eternal feeling broods,
as thought matches the deeper hue –
and spirit dissolves within the dew.

The Touch
Feeling still the ripples,
Your touch sent toward distant lands;
Still the echoes of rapture, lapping
Upon those sacred sands:
That farthest horizon within...
Never known!
Til walking there unalone.

Summerdream
Within that summer night
    Was moonlit madness rolled;
And such measures of delight
    Did savagely unfold,
That those treasures in the night
    Shall ne'er die old.

Deeping Legends of a Purple Land
The forelands of Her eternal dream –
Hills green, wild, and grand –
No lovelier sight in all the deepening
legends of a purple land:

"Here was Tristan, riding
skis in pineleaf haltered
(Rough-fashioned – prone to breakage) –
Riding these slopes, long centuries past,
The Princess in one hand,
cleft pole in another,
'His descent, a lotus, wilting along Acheron
His failing as weepingly Beautiful,
as seemingly Tragic –
As any tale of some young, pondersome Dane.'

Here were Albion, and Hibernia,
for centuries bronzed
In an everlasting twilight's gentle flame;
Here, like thinking trees,

They stood and sang
for twelve thousand years...
Such epic idylls of sweet lyricism,
Such deep lispings – softly so spirituelle.

Tones once trilled by those ancestral sisters
First masters of promethean song:
Breeding athwart the cascading chiliads
Of fast fading foreyears –
The pipings of glories long lost,
The still susurrant chaunt
of distant dreaming seas,
Of empires faint along horizons far glimmering,
Where the very lifestroke
of all breathing nature softly wails
For a scandent Heaven
whose silken strands enfill all space!"

And here lies the noblest feeling,
(though scaresely known to care)
within a sunken dream still reeling
For these brave,
soul-sundered masters of despair.

VI. Passages Parallel
Paired poems, the first in italics and voiced in mostly arcane language; the second, parallel translations in the more common tongue.

A. Dynasties of Artistic Woodland
The rataplan of Her aortal pulse,
Her living oneiria;
The arhat of Duenda;
Ensorcerel lumen flashes geminal
blinked thru palebral maquillage –
Anabases aroll in undulant concatenation,
generations of daedal forest
imbricate distant-dreaming slopes –
What aulic contender for penetrailia anagogic
Dare such contesseration presage?

B. Generations of Daedal Forest
The drumbeat of Her prime artery,
the life in Her dreamworld;
The highest enlightenment of Charm;
What bright spells, from painted eyes
cast and beam?
What successive martial campaigns,
in wave-linking chains,
What dynasties of artistic woodland,
overlay the far, dreaming mountains?

Who of the royal court
dare aspire to these mystic inner chambers
Forespeaking what mad,
beautiful depth of interleaving soul?

A. Alexandra Rustaveli
Her orpharion chords,
an aeonian effluvium of cantabile affusion
transporting us beyond this atrabilious plane.

B. The Danilova Conversion
The music of her lute is an endless flood
of smooth-flowing baptism,
raising us above the flat sadness of Earth.

A. Deathwalk
Discalced, burthened of hame and gyve,
they plodge the barranca, scandent peons –
fraught, maundering
above the harmattan for appeasement
from some necrotic godlet or daemon.

B. The Final March
Barefoot, collared and shackled,
they trudge the muddy ravine, climbing peasants
hopelessly mumbling above the African wind
pale atonements to a god
the young think imaginary or powerless;
and the old see rotting in autumn leaf.

A. Lea
Each oeillade or orison cast upon the delicate
gloriole of her clinquant pantalets:
An astral concatenation of feeling –
Spinning wild on the alpine lea.

B. Mountain Meadow
Each glance or prayer upon the subtle
halo of her glittering underwear frills:
A constellation of sensitivities
above the tantalizing ecstasy
of what mad mountain meadow frolick?

A. Dark, Lidless Constellations
Her mien for fortnights waxed
a darker shade of acheronian murrey,
til the sublime rays cast
from the caliginous asterisms
of her perpending ocelli:
a foehn, fulminant with eldritch
screeds of skald and the verecund
yet quickening sibilance of reclusive lamia –
this chthonic cataclysm,
procellous and nimbus-mantic:
harbinger of Ragnorak in hiemal chiliads.

B. By Mistress Benighted
For seven weeks her countenance accreted
more dark and dismal layers of purple-gray,
until within the grand and terrifying beams
cast from the dark, lidless constellations
of her brooding invertebrate eyes,
arose a suddenly cruel alpine wind
thick with the strange, passionate rantings
of severe Norse poets
and the shy but frightful hissing
of fanciful snake-women;
And this large seeming storm,
this black-shadowed maelstrom
forespeaks a wintry and wolfen Apocalypse
spanning the near ages of futurity.

A. Prinker Brigade
Pullulations of manciple and famuli
tend the overweening prinker
and scrofulous tartuffe...

B. Manciple Revolution
Swarms of stewards
and servants with purchasing authority
pamper the arrogant fancy-dressers
and morally corrupt hypocrites...
until the Revolution.

A. Heather Alpha (Lady o' the Loch)
From near the cromlech, hedged in bosket,
her genuflective orison rolls
across the acheronian moor,
into the spume, and on
for the far, stygian shore.

B. Heather Epsilon (Lass of the Lake)
Near the stone circles, occluded in thicket,
her prayer of submission echoes
o'er the dismal mire,
thru the fine spray,
toward the distant, dream-dark coast.

A. Brumal Moon
'Neath the baldachin of a brumal moon
Their farouche, yet noetic assignation
seems endless as the soul – yet possible,
to the corrading fleer of life's rough passage.

B. Hibernal Canopy
Under the canopy of the wintry moon
Their wild, yet intellectual tryst
feels immortal as the heart's essence
Yet sensitive to the abrading mockery of flesh.

A. The Holy Fire
After fortnights truckled to the furor scribendi
His rooms grew Augean
and mephitic as untended horse stalls.

B. Rage of the Penman
After weeks enslaved
by a madness for passionate composition
The odors of her home grew rich
as if ungulates where stabled therein –
their droppings and effluvia quite neglected.

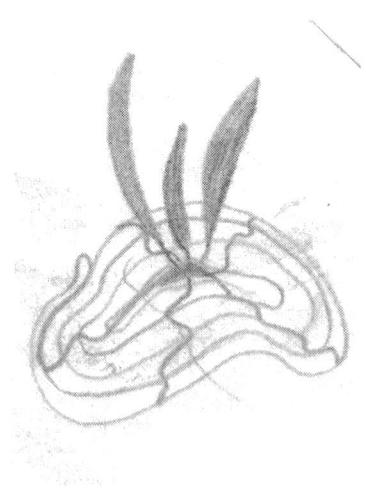

VII. Pale Western Star
Scene 1: Prelusion
Garden of a house party – Julian Stage Left
Julian: [gazing (rapt) offstage]
They said she was lovely, but this...
mortal clay beneath Heaven's kiss
fashioned to o'erwhelm all sense
save the spiritual.
Yearning for her in some new way
(evoking half-dreamt feelings of yesterday)
I must compose within
some love-haunted symphony to win
her camaraderie, and devotion
ere each sublime emotion dissolve
within a loneness too beautiful, too distant –
[Malik approaching from inside the house]
Malik: Julian! Good to see you my friend.
[quieter, almost conspiratorial,
perhaps arm around shoulder]
Now, Julian, your great depression
in our circle is well known –
and a better friend I'd be
to think about you more.
I know you're all right, and yet
disconsolate these last weeks:
so drear an aspect, so dark a shade
your disposition now casts
from the aboriginal glow we who knew you
in its absence come only more to love.

I'm even surprised (pleasantly)
to see you tonight, almost unbidden
at this somewhat random soirée.
Julian: Well, my friend, I freely admit
to harboring the dark
stray thought or two, cast my way
by a seemingly uncaring world;
Perhaps eschewing the brighter ray
my native star beams forth.
Malik: Julian, I know,
this last romantic breakage...
Julian: Yes, difficult... the memory of joy –
if only hope would just die...
[a deliberative pause.]
But she's across the sea, forever lost to me
never returning to these blessèd lands
I call home and cannot forsake: not for a year,
nor for one aestival season. Heavy the chain
upon those thoughts of what once was...
Malik: So why not follow for *half* a season?
Julian: It's not a land
Within which I countenance living.
But no matter, Malik,
for tonight we're unalone;
With friends abounding
I see what hope remains...
[Gaze turns]
And on seemingly unrelated note
I beg your gaze to fall

upon that far corner, and the strange lass,
who, residing there – eyes feral,
(blonde, on leather),
doth cast her look – o so subtly
from time to time in our general direction.
(Or am I so transported from all reason
to rightly discern such an overture?)
[shaking off any doubts]
No, my friend, it matters not:
an instinct almost divine
informs the chase –
her charm-enraptured glance
demands she be pursued –
and if by chance, I find myself
graced beneath her fancy's gaze,
intenser dreams may launch
a braver sky...its fresh gold sun –
(Already I paint in ethereal hue!)
And yes...I will – I *must* pursue!
Malik: She's as sure and lovely
as you are touched
by that which you don't understand!
This strange woman, unknown
perplexes at each greater strangeness,
the crass motion your naked soul
feels compelled to unmask.
Why streak down her central park
with no deference to allow
an approach of one's own volition? –

She's Daphne, fleeing you
and just before the snare
roots beneath her feet are sprouting,
as her limbs to greenwood turn,
(that moss was once her hair!)
And that's the last you see of her:
Love, my friend – more distant now than ever.
Julian: You know me better than I myself
seeing me with eyes on
nothing closer than that horizon
lying blue beyond far, green hills;
but now I'll tell you, Malik, of the wealth
of the rainbow-gold I find out there:
tis better to follow your selfish bliss
than do without and pretend to share.
I mean to pursue her, even without
examining those things we weep about.
Malik: Such romantic madness
toward sad desolation leads –
poetic, perhaps, but surely set apart
too far for ever any human heart
to feel life's Oneness;
There *is* communion – the thing exists:
a promise to balance your seeming bliss.
Julian: I sense the truth you speak
yet sensing more, more inward weep
from eyes that see but one:
(yon golden lass, fresh from the sun!)
About to leave, yet lingering still

as if in wonder how such a place
might lift her hope past loneliness.
And I too linger, but soon
will yearn to wander beneath the moon
to stalk the pine-darkened vale,
to pray upon the light
of mountain glory upon midnight height –
enkindling the quest for more beautiful lives.
And so must I now approach.
[walks toward Mysterious Beauty]
Malik: Naught else you could do, I suppose
so wild your thoughts, ranging the throes
of so "sweet and strange a madness" –
seeping from a mind that knows
the crest-wilted dregs of bitter yearning...
No, I am too harsh: you're living
proof of a soul that's more than giving
and find a way to lift those spirits
most akin to thine endeavor –
endeavor one could not explain
lest he wrote a tome in words of pain
with tears unteaching all ye knew;
But still...[looks over and calls to him] Julian!
[shrugging and muted] Why pursue?
[Vida approaching from offstage]
Vida: Malik, old friend, how goes?
Where's Julian?
Malik: [motioning to the keg, which Julian tends]
Indeed where? – not even he knows.

[pointing offstage]
Claims to be approaching her though.
Vida: [looking] Who is she? Do you know her?
Malik: No, she just stands there... alone.
Vida: How is our friend
and the *montane melancholia*
he seems to almost cherish of late?
Malik: Unchanged. Tho there seems
life in him yet...
Vida: Does he think chasing
this new feline will improve his feeling?
Seems the unknown alone allures him.
Malik: Her beauty may at least *distract* his pain.
[arching brows] Not knowing better,
I'd say a lady was trending jealous...
Vida: That's preposterous!
Malik: Yes, as preposterous as he ever liking *you*.
Vida: What? He's never fancied me.
Malik: No matter. Better this
than some slow depressive smolder
I suppose. [They watch as the scene ends.]

Scene 2: Twilight Encounter

Still in the garden at the house party
Julian: [Approaching Mysterious Beauty]
My dear, I greet you, perhaps you would
consider a walk – it's understood
that kindness may motivate desire
(yet expectation not steal futurity's fire) –

So why not walk with me?
Why not bathe within the mystery
until these waters, stars and trees
"weave a spell of secret courage
On they who brave the *dark and deep*,
Rather than follow sinking suns to sleep"?
Mysterious Beauty:
You "quote in classic raptures"
words I half forgot I knew
when transport, and passing laughters
were to my life, satiety.
(Yet the boreal night shall not encroach
til August upon these lands!)
[gazing about as if suddenly
seeing the world thru new eyes]
This party, this earth, this mystic summer light:
leading toward what, I wonder?
[aside] (And if there's lightning,
will there be thunder?)
[as if shaken from deep ponderings]
Please...you may call me Christine.
Julian: Christine, Julian. I guess, you...
see what I mean?
Christine: Yeah, why not?
Why outlive a time grown too stale?
Julian: Why linger...
Where no one's left to flirt with.
Christine: [soft aside]
(Or no feeling's left to hurt with.)

I'll just leave my bike, so we can talk.
Julian: No need Christine: I too rode here
I'll just grab my cloak and one last beer;
And o'er the twilight we ride
teasing the pale eye of summer's eve
toward opening at close of day.
Christine: Two larks awing toward a second sun
forgetting the days of youth are done.
[suddenly somber] Youth...At the noon of its day
dancing down the flowered slope –
I fell, just half-believing the strange way
my ankle twisted and snapped,
(the gods mocking a strident urge toward play?)
So now, half-halt, I know
the days of dance are gone...
I take the chance to ride
and, free of limp, with cyclonic stride
I find a freedom... I forget to hide
those most beautiful things about me.
I ride, and, as in dance, find a glee
that nourishes –
a sweet and eternal nourish for me.
Julian: Of course – you love to ride, as do I
(what kinship may here we find?)
The mysterious joy – riding the day away
along these strange travels,
we call life – And may I further say
that with a certain grace you move;
an angel with nothing left to prove

whispering the spell of her beauty.
Christine: Sir, you rave half-mad – we just met
and at a party no less, sharing a beer:
it's not like we trekked for months in Thibet! –
(and you've not even seen me ride!)
What about me could you like *so* much?
Julian: You have a body I'd love to touch
and in your face such beauty find –
Christine: [playfully petulant]
What of my wit, my sparkle, my... elegant mind?
Julian: *They're all quite nice, and surely entice*
(to their merits I'll never be blind)
but your body's a deluge of passionate thought
and your face fills me with a pain that ought
to kill were it not too beautiful.
Christine: You're a passionate, yet pathetic one
for seeming so easily overcome
by the "deluge" of a moment's beauty.
Julian: [turning toward the horizon]
A moment's beauty – nay!
Perhaps thus it was perceived, yet
bred ten-thousand years and a day,
such beauty from your soul projects,
with color and shape to express
each forgotten lifetime of loveliness...
Christine: Is that what you see?
When you gaze at the sky,
[mocking] so poetic, so...distantly.
[too suddenly serious, and a bit distant herself]

I wish I shared that bliss
interlacing this world's ugliness...
But enough already! Do we ride, or no?
Julian: [aside] Why toward petulance
Do so oft the lovelier trend?
[They exit and begin riding]

Scene 3: "This Ride Was My Delight"
Julian: Riding...yes, we go a journey
Looking for what? We do not worry
lest the wishful thing flee
or melt beneath too eager a gaze.
Cycling, we watch; talking, we feel –
here we live without reflection,
each moment one fresh draught
of what the universe thinks we ought
to be feeding our souls. And be this pain –
or pleasures too rough and wild to contain
is no choice for us, but for Destiny a dream:
Cast forever beyond what we seem.
Christine: Hah! To the pond,
there is some depth
rippling beneath the brute mess
of your formless life.
There lies an edge I can't dismiss
casting its shade of lifefulness
upon those things more precious
to the soul and body than breath –
could we unearth them whole,

(before... or even after death)
What beauty could we know?
What bliss from lost horizons' glow?
Julian: Quite the Romantic eh?
yours a life too sweet and strange,
as if, wishing a moment more,
beyond the last Creation
the eternal Universe forever threw
aside every rule it ever knew –
to bud the thornless rose,
to emancipate with beauty
without shackling in pain.
Christine: And you're even more the dreamer
(forever nourished by fairy visions)
whose heart faints near conscious thought;
knowing too little of other creatures:
forever stamped apart
from humankind as surely thou art –
a freak none may understand.
Julian: Well! I take that insult as the most
divine of sentiments ever a host
dared to express;
for what I am so gladdens me
I never care how it maddens the
masses of humanity.
And you too of alter spirit bent
perhaps can see, or hear it lent
to the wind that blows a cloud of dream
across this sky of azurine...

[silence, then nonchalant, with a jaded tinge]
Ah, the park...and there's the swing.
[They mount separately and swing together]
Christine: Yes, what delight! Here we move;
Julian: Yet go nowhere, not needing to prove –
Christine: We have some purpose,
for deep inside
our breathing souls, where hearts can hide;
Julian: In a land peopled by two, we reign,
over glorious empires that rise...
     and fall again,
lasting perhaps not beyond the moment.
So, yes, let's swing:
Let's love what we're wasting!
[She moves onto neighboring grass –
he gently pursues.]
Julian: [Looking at her as if upon
a scene of alien visitation]
You're a strange one indeed...
your thoughts as wild as the lips they reach;
[aside] I most wonder: is her touch
as wild and strange as her speech?
Christine: You, my friend, are a calamitous flirt!
I've wisdom enough to stow feelings from hurt
so rendering myself insensitive to charm.
Julian: Insensitive you seem, yet soon may yield,
sensing no harm could occur on this field
beneath a moon so calm.
This night, this moment, the park, the trees:

all scream for submission – and you Christine?
Release some feeling, or the chance may pass...
Christine: The chance? For what?
For kisses? Or feelings just as transitory?
To taste what knows
the pleasure of things that will not last?
The chance for bliss to enfold our woes
within layers we think we touch,
til clouds linger pink above
the eternal hope for all lasting love –
The chance to feel alive forever!...
But no! bliss outspends its own endeavor:
A once passionate heart, now riven, tattered
will moan of love as all that mattered –
madly reeling from all that would
seek forever the inextinguishable good
of a passion ne'er to be repeated.
Julian: Tis true: love's a risky affair
opening its rose only to those who dare
pursue a glory that may come to grief.
Yet if She, like you, were fully aware
fully awake to the *possible* in life,
surely the danger subsides in proportion
surely (balanced in resistance),
love tempers itself toward lasting existence?
Christine: Julian, your discourse
is the vilest distortion!
As if love opposed is lengthened!
No power can weaken, nor strengthen

contract nor extend
the breadth of love, the depth
to which this force penetrates a soul.
Were Love entire bound within the stroke
of lightning upon the midnight oak
there She'd find eternity.
Julian: Precisely! When love streams down,
– beams from above
into the oracle of passionate man –
Christine: [Dreamy, as if in deep remembrance]
Love becomes her breath
deprived of which, she lives in death;
And if upon some golden lass,
the touch of love comes swift and light;
she laughs, then cries –
then feels this must
become a heaven, high above
this lost mortality, this unearthly love:
a paradise of soft-pillowed sighs –
and here she frolics, or here she dies.
"And will he leave," she wonders;
"and could I live, would there be such
a thing to call my love, would breath
still steam our morning skin, would life
still funnel its joy against the tide of strife?"
Julian: For men its different,
yet of course, the same
(these players who play, yet alone remain),
stray-eyed Don Juan-a-bes

masquerading as Kings –
A paper-thin paradise,
blackened with one desire.
Christine: The question for woman is:
Can she trust this fire?
This man whose passion seems it must
express itself within the throes
of such idealized phantasy?
To wing from Earth to such a world
risking all upon a lark – beautiful, perhaps;
But will this feeling perch for long
or wing across the seas? Will her nest
be blown apart, or find eternal rest?
Julian: Are not all things that promise great gain
fraught with possibility for pleasure...
and for pain?
Life is meant to be boldly lived:
to complete one's soul, even if on Earth
love perished from the pain of another birth
still wouldst we strive, for that bliss we feel
is ours by the right of our pain to heal
to grasp for greatest happiness.
As husband and wife first meeting
(strangers jostling an awkward greeting);
Like the hart hunted not for meat –
love hath neither rhyme nor reason
but to be pursued *in season*.
Christine: [Contemplating his wit,
yet aware of his limitation]

Your mind is a path
leading toward a setting sun,
whose fading beauty forces you to shun
the good and lasting things this land hath
laid open to more open eyes.
Julian: My gaze is fixed, my eyes are laid
upon as lovely horizon shade
as ever was perceived:
And still its reality eludes me.
I wonder, How this could be?
How, dreamt beneath the twilight gleaming
the spires' purpureal hues
do speak to the Muse –
And if this vision you invoke
then who am I to pretend I've woke?
Christine: [playing along, for now]
Life's song continues, we the strings
plucked by a Hand whose motion brings
the greatest euphony out of pain.
And so what if the song begins again?
Julian: A song, never ending
an eternal chorus, forever blending
what we know with what we dream.
Christine: So... why?
Julian: Why run to destruction
when our savior's at hand?
Dismissing reason to believe in a sigh?
We make our fate, weave our plan
(as true for saint as for common man):

I'd rather drown in sweet seas
than starve on dry land.
Christine: Lovers of Destiny,
– we cannot turn back
each possessing what the other may lack;
Not granted to either is strength to repel
this love we live – a fated spell!
Delivering unto Heaven...
before sentencing to Hell?
Julian: Yes, it's possible we'll find
our future selves wracked in pain
wishing hard not to live again;
but if *now* is all the chance we have
why not accept what joy
a knowing universe may offer?
Christine: Your logic is moving, but I've a heart
grown unrelenting as if a part
of it still cries for death
such from its hurt still recovering.
So I'll not mount your heaving steed
nor ride with wondering desire
(borne upon some ephemeral fling) –
nor burn in the momentary fire
Romantic sickeners already enkindle...
Julian: Such the passion you reject –
but, whatever...I still respect
the reason that ranks along your defense...
[two beats] But *come*, let's go
toward where fields lie in snow;

a route I've marked between the firs,
up the steep acclivity –
Come, we outfly the sun
frolicking twilight into day
as dawn lights the higher reaches;
Just pausing for breath, raptured away,
we scale the forested cliff;
To explore a lovely, secret place –
where finger and tongue
may unleash the pleasures they taste.
[pondering faint summer stars as much as her.]
Christine: All right already!
I'm *potentially* interested, I suppose.
Where lies this secret place?
Julian: Just over the hill, to the second bridge
turn left, then follow the ridge
up through the forest and past the falls,
and there's our mountain nest –
high among moss and trees,
(above purple seas!)
we'll take our rest.
Christine: I'll hike to your nest,
knowing you didn't
intend such strong inclinations
toward pressing *advanced* relations.
I like you, surely I do!
But this is too strange:
this meeting, this...thrust – I still wonder
who on Earth you are?

Allow some time for understanding
and approach not in over-confident guise.
Julian: I stand chastened...
But for *now* let's climb
while still the twilight deepens!
[Fade out]

Scene 4: Upon Aeried Heights
Lightening upon a green bower, the sun just rising behind a peak across the water. They sit together, but do not touch.
Christine: A sublime view indeed!
Eclipsing the need
to feast on mortal beauty;
for here we see, the love that'd be,
if humans could *truly* understand each other.
Julian: For Nature provides
a mirror that never lies,
where we see our selves as we could be –
grand, golden, free,
and independent of mortality.
[several seconds silence]
Christine: Such a lovely height!
It makes one wish – we almost might...
[she looks at him – he's looking out to sea.]
Julian: Eyes upsweep the vast spacing
from ocean to hill, mountain to sky
connecting nature with meaning, almost erasing
the pang of mortal birth.

And in such beauty death
seems almost a thing with breath –
How easy to just breathe so deeply in
[does so and holds] –
[exhaling] Then dive over the edge
to live once again!
[He leaps, and, grabbing a branch
projecting o'er the abyss, hangs by one arm.]
Christine: [taking his audacity
somewhat in stride]
I've felt that same wish
and romanticized the precipice –
But please! – can you stop messing around?
Julian: [swings back to her side]
Come! let's run
let's dive into bliss!
From here to the edge
of this strange wilderness –
Come, let's fly
let's dare with our dreams
to feel as real as if the streams
of heaven herself lay open unto us!
Christine: Streams of Heaven or rivers of Hell?
I'm not too sure I'd even shag you
let alone follow your leap from life –
The former's path I see too well
and of the latter, too little.
So how could I? –
Surely I'll not so yield my soul.

Julian: *It's not your soul must yield*
nor heart, nor hips;
It's only a snuggle I need –
to tease the wild nerve:
a little pressing flesh
to remind the human years.
Christine: From love, to death... to frottage!
[sadly, she shakes her head]
your mind's a wandering shade,
your body struggling
to climb out its material skin.
So why not spare us *the withering desire*?
For surely "...to be wise *and* love
is hardly granted to gods above."
Julian: In youth one images a destiny
(unique, glorious – tinged in poesy) –
One ponders up some Great Golden She
to smooth the wrinkle of mortality –
Then years pass, and looking at life:
without emotion, no faith to feel –
We wither, as if too tired to heal
this strange disease of modern living...
And what's the escape?
Something drastic it'd seem:
we were not meant for this sorrow,
not born to this dream.
Christine: If you taste too much of sorrow
then ponder an unknown tomorrow –
and those days of passing sun:

You were happy then just to live!
How much more glad you'd be
really *feeling* what it might mean?
[long silence, little motion –
eyes upon the ocean]
Julian: Another vision rises that we could share:
A distant land, golden spires cast
a purple glow – the sinking sun,
of deeper hue than our pale western star –
sand, rock and secret tribes: life aflame
in romantic quests for glory.
Such a place we could find, surely –
if only the resolve to muster,
to leave all we've ever known
pursue a dream, "the substance of faith";
Gathering needful things,
pack, cloak, and boot
gifting the rest... slowly, not as to shock
those whom we love – then wave subtle,
but forever deep farewells;
and one day, wake and flee
with words to none.
Across mountain, lake, forest and sea
(guided by unseen hand)
toward some deep desert mystery –
never to return.
Christine: "Tis distance
lends enchantment to the view,
and robes the mountain in its azure hue"

– life always felt too close
so you wished beyond the horizon
to worship a thing
too sweet & strange for living –
And now think fleeing across the seas
or leaping off the edge
will somehow fix everything?
It's madness, really.
Julian: [moving to sit by her]
I am feeling a tad touched –
just vertiginous from the height, I suppose.
Christine: This is no sudden fever
nor quick flash from crazèd eye –
but slow-brewed for years [looks into his eyes]
and lost in the swell of inward tears –
Surely you *are* touched! ...and from deep within.
Julian: [Playing along, perhaps]
Fay and sprite calling from the trees...
leaping shapes and voices –
A wondrous world swirls inside,
[gesturing first toward his head, then the sea]
and now seeps toward the world without.
I am living alone, as if no Censor
sniffs what may smoke still
from the Church within my head;
beneath its dreaming spire I kneel,
seeking wisdom from the dead, the will
and reality toward which we conspire
seeps from me,

to wreathe the funeral pyre –
And in the seeping, sours. [pause]
Yet behold this wide world –
A blessèd early summer morn
upon the aeried heights high-borne!
The sky ablaze, the trees, the park far below
just here beneath the last pink line of snow...
Christine: [long silence.] It's lovely, as you say,
as charming as you in some strange way.
[Julian's head nestles upon her lap –
and with hands through hair,
past eyes that only stare
the passing cumuli enchant them.]
Julian: What is human happiness, I wonder?
What distant hopes, what half-forgotten dreams?
What fragile, sympathetic whimperings?
What love, what natural way of seeing?
I know not, and yet some felicity
these companionable moments find –
though you remain heavy of spirit.
If there's a why or what-for, I'd love to hear it?
[another pause]
Christine: There was one, like you perhaps –
so *unencumbered* –
who pursued me.
Not too frantic nor subtle was he;
but with sweetly measured words and look
he championed my soul.
Later, much later, our feverheads touching

he matched what my own heart mistook
for love. Three years we lived, passionately
with a force like the sun I was blind to see
what from shadow moons unfolded –
Then suddenly...(but no, twas gradual)
he broke with me
blaming a fault I could not perceive.
Shattered, I wander this half year
another love so far from mind.
I craved only death, phantasizing the blade
self-propelling soul to grave:
Without him life was meaningless.
I yearned; I prayed; I worshipped the shade –
yet still felt condemned to live;
I read Byron's *Manfred*,
weeping the rogue hero's rage!
I stopped reading Shelley –
and Baudelaire became a waste of page...
Still I wander, the hope of life returning, slowly
and gently, the feelings... and with feeling –
perhaps yearning? [two beats]
I just want something new to feel –
some *raison d'etre*!?
Julian: Yeah, I know what you mean:
sometimes life isn't quite real
and you run and scream, and steal
the moments from a godless plane;
Then awaken, walking again
into the stream of human life:

The masses, strangers, and stranger places
you'll never see, frothing
in some mad teaming sea
of endless, raving humanity... [pause]
For me too there was one
a friend I'd known for years.
We danced and played and roamed the hills;
We read and wept, sharing dreams
and probed each other's inner beings –
Then passed a golden age
of empathetic days.
We loved those weeks and months
(she as much me), though knowing,
more than friends we'd never be.
Already too lost in love,
and soon unable to see her
the pain too deep, my actions imbalanced
by every hope to mount a deeper alliance.
Being with her was full, rich, divine –
even the love of friends of old
seemed a thin shadow cast behind
the beaming sun of her presence.
Months passed, then years – but even now
seeing her, by chance, with friends
returns me *within*, feeling
the trust & rapport, the communal depth –
equaled only in the hope of years
now vanished, seemingly forever.
Christine: So what if you're a wanderer,

a lone wolf, an Amazon without a tribe?
When you feel most alone
when "lashed upon a midnight moan"
you dream across the ocean and seas
aloft the passionate breeze –
a vision too wild for actual life.
Obviously a man of *honor*
(though struggling against his needs)
you wish to pounce *upon her*
whilst dreaming of what she'll be –
A truth you'll never see, but live
on sunlight & nectar gleaming
along her silver throat –
the beauty of unborn angels singing,
as down from heaven she's streaming,
whispering dreams of the dead
as rich and satiate as noontide sun
while deepening love's fullest desire –
Surely a vision worthy only one
so deep within life's "holy fire."
Julian: You mock me
somehow pretending I have a choice
not to dream – to love only just
what before these eyes is thrust?
Creativity's fled: the holy fire spent
no more whispering dreams from the dead –
and without these, how can I live?
What can I do?
Christine: You've dreamt enough, my friend

so what if those visions fade?
Reality can be fun! You should try it;
Start living, reinvigorate –
whilst considering the universal fate:
"Dreamers! See the present need!
Through the whirlwind flies your seed"
unnourished. And so one must calm
the winds of madness,
and cease tempting ill fate.
Return to Character... reinvigorate!
Julian:
[without standing, swings legs over the abyss]
Your speech is moving, as much
for tenderness as for truth;
Yet I cannot move away, but feel
surely tis my right, should I choose
to quench this fire here on earth:
To force the spark of another birth
perhaps beneath some distant star.
God may choose when I'm born
cannot man choose when to die?
Christine: No, you arrogant little thing!
Surely you may not! Not even so much
as one may dare
to choose the time of loving. [pause]
Julian: Well, what about now?
Here, alone, in no more perfect place –
Why not... yield to each other?
Together, now, so painlessly

fleeing our souls but forgetting to flee
our thoughts in tune with the summer moon
we'll hurl into the blue
diving deep until we almost knew–
Christine: This passes for wooing these days?
This...sacrificial enticement?
Julian: What [moving closer] more [closer]
can I offer? [They kiss.]
Mid the breath of a thousand
swirling sighs we linger –
Yet even the first flowers of foresight
see Love's countenance
for but a modest stretch of life;
And, besides, there seems an inner strife
an unknown war
that could end our happiness...
Christine: Julian, what on Earth –
Julian: [standing and breaking in]
You see, Christine, I have a choice
of two paths, the one out there
[points into the abyss]
the other within myself;
And the inner, of course
is also the outer: to flee this place,
in hope some foreign land may spur
a new life, a fresh passion of soul.
To find the strength to finish proper
what could've been – what *should've* been –
a much finer life...

and yet was not.
At least this way we'll always love
[he's looking toward the abyss]
and our beauty never fade.
Christine: No, you mustn't!
No matter the challenge,
stay and strive, overcome your daemons
pursue due course, no matter the pain
or anguish, or what madness may come.
Return now! – you need not explain
fully yourself. But step from the abyss:
For Heaven's sake, Julian!
Julian: [Holding his precipitous pose]
I'm sorry my dear, that I cannot do
for time is short, but pain long
consuming all we've ever been –
to ashes with every hoped for thing!
No, it must end here, upon these heights... only
Do I have eyes for such a leap?
[he looks down, then turns to jump]
Farewell, sweet sister of fate!
Christine: Wait, stay! Together we'll go
to the distant land:
The purple dreaming spires beneath
an evening star of purer tone.
We'll slip away, as you like –
Just alone we two, and in that loneness
Who knows what healing find?
It's a chance for life – Why refuse?

Julian: [stepping over, clasping her wrist]
The distant land appeals;
Yet cannot [abyss-ward motion] this way we go?
Death is a deeper traveling ...

Scene 5: Epilog
[Malik and Vida, in the park, by the swings]
Malik: Last seen conversing with her:
Beautiful, despite attendant daemons,
apparent to me and others,
but to Julian unseen.
She remains unknown to us –
and neither's been sighted
these three days passed:
Presumed dead – or forever lost.
Vida: And that unknown *she*,
appearing and leaving just as soon
as Julian would from parties of seasons past.
That night she spoke to none else, apparently;
Such fleet sightings:
our only proof she was real?
Malik: [museful] His a life spent
before actually lived,
his treasure, gilding horizons never ventured.
Vida: After the party,
someone's spoken (or thought?) sighting,
of Julian here [pointing],
alone near the water wheel,
by the trail up high steeps – we know

He finds pleasure there often...
I fear, climbing that night, with her, or alone
She or he – or both... fell?
Malik: I've known him better than most
and yet, secrets he harbored,
dreams, fears – quiet pains.
But his sureness of foot, I cannot doubt,
we having played upon those same sheer slopes
a thousand nights before.
I slipped a time or two – but never he.
Vida: What if he were pushed?
Malik: [scoffs] Why?
Vida: Or jumped?
Malik: [pause] Well, his mood
was melancholic of late, but...
Vida: Yes, he was prone
to post-solstice melancholia.
Malik: And equinotic euphorias, yes,
that's well-documented –
but still, he couldn't have....
Vida: You're right. Never. Perhaps he finally ran
off to the Tartusian lands...
like he sometime hinted –
without even saying good-bye?
Malik: Yes, just a sudden, missed at work,
not friends, nor family calling,
but sending letters from abroad. [pause]
Perhaps....and she with him? –
Across the oceans, through desert,

running "Anywhere Out of the World"?
So taken by her, so clear and primal:
"Faceted within that rainbow sphere –
A sunlit soul, a feeling tear?"
Vida: [gazing up-mountain]
We'll miss you, old friend. And forgive your kissless leave,
sans wave, sans note, sans noble wishes.
We hope you live... and love, but... why?
Why leave these who loved you most?

The End

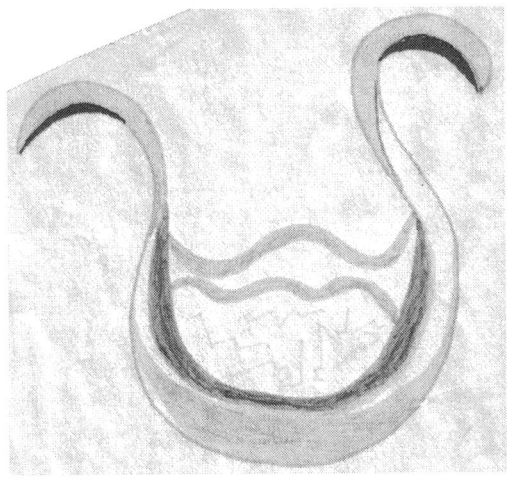

VIII. Seven Hills Ski Park Chart

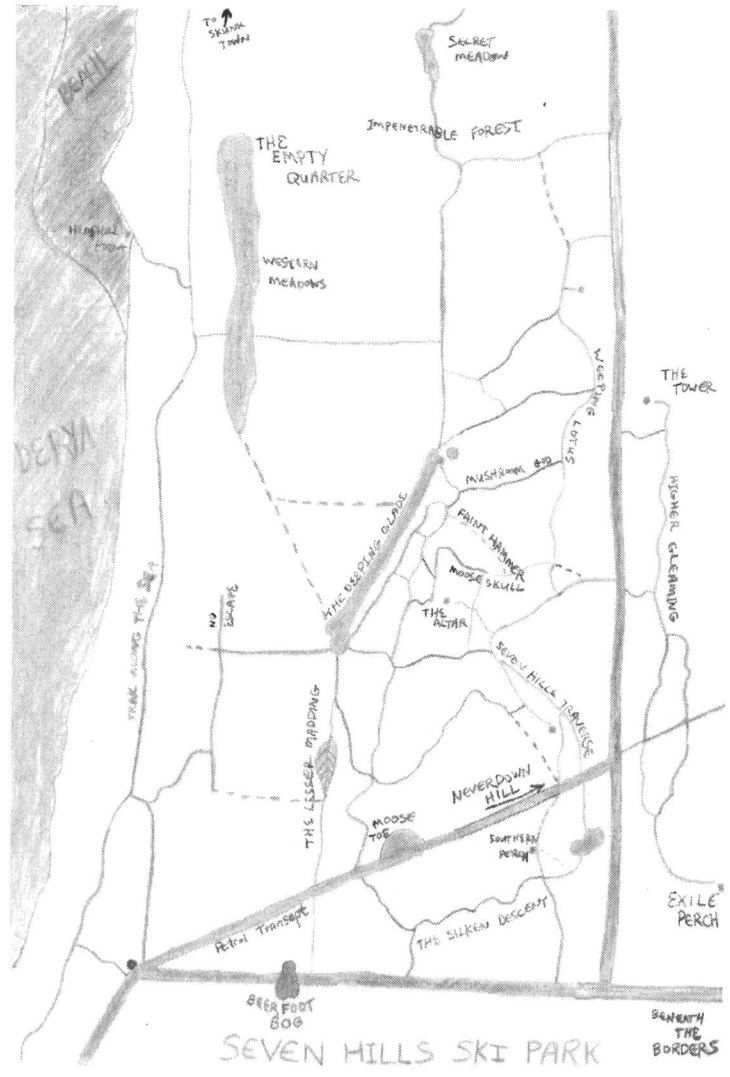

IX. The Neverlands

The Southern Flanks are opening,
the high perches set,
the half-meter storm's a'waned;
and azurine skies prevail upon the main.
(Strings of passing cumuli –
Lay dormant as the last true lumens die.)
The snows as deep, the birch as bright,
the glide of pole, pack and ski
ride along the southern sea
toward what hidden sundoven mystery?

Upon sun-split slopes of ice and spray
Mushroom God's an easy pull
as we breach these sacred hills –
and up Weeping Lotus, still we stride
toward the Higher Perch
to catch the view from Seventh Hill.
and taste the Higher Gleaming –
Then down The Chute and thru the trees
(neglecting neither Moose Toe nor Grabtree)
edging The Declivity, onto Second Mound
we linger, drinking sweet knowledge...
Then up the Neverdown, we dare
To wind the Silken Descent! And north, turning
to crest the Toe, we coast
into the Deeping Glade, toward the Firecircles.

And here were God's Own Friends
with ski and sled and spouts of wine
with packs and snacks, rope and thread
on boarded or saucered-feet,
riding spike-cycles,
sliding, hiking, gliding – with falls
skiing, or sledding – with poles, from perches
mid song, dance, and drink
in series along the meadow's edge –
some skating, glissading, or shuffling along
all thru the golden melt of Spring.

The Primatrix climbs in light purple skins
toward the grace of the plunge
on The Silken Descent!
And the Likely Lads on their haltered skis;
and Truth's Own Daughters in the trees –
(casting their thoughts and shattering dreams);
And Puella, near the Altar, capering
above the meadow's slight declivity –
and The Virga Dawn still wanders on
through the glorious, sun-gilded leas...
And mid this paradise of dreaming gods
we think our way thru the Empty Quarters
to the Trail Along the Sea...

X. LOST TUVAN PRINCESS
Canto One: Party of Forgotten Laughtering
Chorus: *From the greeting room,*
thru passage unseen;
down oaken hall past portals clear:
The deck – above a sounding stream:
views sublime of wood, rock, and glacier tongue.
Robin sees her, beneath pink cloud
seeming alone, mid moss and trees
along the rail, gazing far
upon the pale yellow sky-borne breeze;
Auburn hair blown o'er an olive face
her lips the light pink of the chaste;
The eyes, turning, rise in smoldered burning –
so intense a countenance
she cast, he wants to look askance –
(o'er-whelmed in conflated feeling
of destinies and deja vus)
He beats the urge and, nearly quailing
holds the glance – at once she softens:
bright coals of green
crumbling to embered dream.
Shapur: Robin, if you please, meet Neko:
We met last March, on the Illyrian Traverse
Without food was I, but she was worse
having snapped a tibia in descent.
We shared her food as I drug us free
for miles thirty and three:
A fair exchange we both agreed.

And Neko – Robin I've known
since roaming these fields as youth
And these [waves hand at the hills] slopes skiing
ten-thousand times while at the academy.
And now, please excuse me,
I'm wanted here, but elsewhere wanted more.
[Shapur exits to the study]
Robin: Neko, lovely to see you... I wonder
if inquiring after the lineage
producing such a visage
would seem an opening unfit?
Neko: They call me Neko,
but my true name's India
(though never having lived in that land);
My Tuvan grandmother's father was a Kurd
and she mated a Kazahk in Govi;
My mother they bore, and she married a Turk
only to die with me on her teat
in Dushanbe, where we lived when he left
Smilova to fight the East Pamiri wars
from which he never returned.
[pause – unspoken empathy]
And from what stock have you sprung?
Robin: Golgothic-Arctican, mostly,
perhaps with a Shambhalese pinch in the brew.
Neko: I'm fairly certain no such lineage exists!
[they both laugh, then ponder the sunset]
Robin: A singular evening, yes?
[waving his hand casually

at the myriad glories attendant in visible nature]
What with the gloaming horizon and all...
Neko: *"They ne'er betide set, in spring, nor winter to slumber, nor sweeten more,*
than leafy hills of sundown glinter."
[Perfect, was her rendering / the verse weightless
upon the twilight for moments tendering]
Robin: Hmm... Those lines I can't quite place –
Western Boreal? Maybe Kashatok? Or Karakum!
A tortured fragment
from one of his "Fallow Phases"?
Neko: [with a perhaps patronizing smile]
Nay Boreal, nor mere fragment
and Kashatok may only dream
of penning such loveliness!
From whose quillage could such an idyll issue?
Only Petra. Luna. Cumulus.
(No greater poet in any age or realm)
Her signature coda no less
from *Cycles of Cumuli*.
In the third act, the King
recalls a vision from yestreen
of his death in battle upon the morrow
as he spied the hills at twilight
he could just glimpse from the Tower
where much of his youth he languished...
And Karakum? [playful] I could scarsely stay
at party – In fact,
I would actively flee for solitude

were I to mistake Petra for Karakum!
Robin: Apologies, my lady:
Shame to a good Boreal
but I've not read the *Cycles*
for years on years.
Yet, especially in youth, oft I did rely
upon verse to buoy my soul
beyond the mundane –
perhaps much like that King
and his twitterlit reverie.
At any rate, considering your lineage it seems
you've a story or two to tell
of lands I've not dreamed.
Neko: For sure, I do, some other night
or after the light fades, perhaps.
It seems we've met before?
You say those lands you've only dreamt –
Yet I think in Govi, Tuva, or near the Preserve
some half-remembered time –
A friend's friend that I met but once?
Or encountered alone perhaps?
In the greenwood, the Barrens,
or among the Dunes?
Robin: My whole life
the Boreal lands I've roamed
of Eastern Arctica, my ancestral home;
Venturing toward southern hills a time or two –
but never to the Tuvan Realm,
nor around the Sea.

It's not so large a country, yet
one could easily lifetimes spend
richly exploring only it.
Neko: Strange...I remember
a caravan upon the sand,
bound by night to avoid patrols;
between the rocks, in shadow, if a moon:
Our goal so distant we actively chose
to risk the lingering light of day
rather than dare an open dawn –
a mistake too soon rued indeed...
But that was long ago, another world.
Robin: Why do you travel
the Western Boreal now, my lady?
Neko: I loved a Boreal Turk – a smuggler;
He'd gather me in Tartus,
and we'd sail the lonesome Astrid Coast
to his island fastness.
There, one night, upon the parapets of stone,
a cliff-fall aloft relentless breakers
mid a storm, he proposed to me...
[She is almost wholly transported, eyes
upon the world's farther shore.]
They called him Altan (meaning "dawn"
in the early tongue). [heavy pause]
I was advisor, Cambridge-credentialed
to a noble king;
for many years we lived, and well
between the island and the Palace at Tartus

(first city of Boreal Turkistan).
Suddenly (and yet was gradual no doubt – tho
we saw not the impending political danger)
a pretender seized the throne
he was false, pitiless, and terrible.
But that was all so long ago...
[Silence prevails for a moment only
then, so fast, her weary sheen vanishes –
alert, she circles to Robin's other side.]
The air grows suddenly cool –
perhaps you fancy a steam?
Robin: [puzzled, but not overly hesitant]
Why not? This way, my dear.
[Slight tension from Neko, but they walk
casually toward the hothouse offstage.]

Canto Two: High Meadows Cabin
Neko: A lovely after sauna ski –
I'm most enervated, but pleasantly!
Robin: "After sauna?" We hardly broke sweat
And you rushed us here. "Pleasantly enervated?"
Well I'm bloody-well knackered!
These 30 klicks over the hills –
[he looks at her, head shaking]
So fast you move – and I thought myself
somewhat able.
Were you once Ski Meister or what?
Neko: I was 3 seconds from bronze
in Shambhala

and 5.2 from victory at Smilova;
Tho I did triumph once
in the Orcadian Shambles.
Do you know it?
A great nordic challenge
based on Norwegian legends of Norse kings,
Runeberg & Frode, the frontier of whose lands
lay just beyond the Shambles –
where ice, heaped in riven crumbles
height upon steeping height –
A mass of glacier, crag, and peak,
choked with crevasse and abyssia.
Then Runeberg, surprised by a hundred Turkmen
was nearing retreat when Frode
following secret routes
arrives with but four friends
(skiers from the royal team –
none else able to match his pace).
Using the land and hidden controls
various traps they sprung
to direct Avalanche & Flood;
Then darting some 20
with blowtube and bow;
They cast off skis at castle, just as Runeberg
slayed the offending royal.
Victory secured, in those sweet
spring lands they lingered
skiing the crust with Runeberg and his knights
a full fortnight before Frode's return.

And every year, after the Transept race
the fabled fortnight's festivity relives.
Those two weeks, after capturing gold
stretch now in memory like a silver tower
of time 6 months building.
That's where I met *Her*...
[as if shaken awake]
Oh, yes, and one season
I won the Interlaken tour –
But again, all years ago
(do pardon the digression).
Robin: Quite alright my dear;
But, please, finish the story of your flight
interrupted earlier by our own.
Neko: Altan could not countenance
the terrible rule of the new king;
and after his coup failed
in Middle Govi they soon found me.
Barely escaping, months in the wind, til I reached
the Dunes of the Waning Crescent;
and met an allied tribe in the western foothills.
That first spring, a nordic paradise I found
matched only by its aestival's sister beauty.
Many bright weeks,
for long sun-slanting forenoons
we'd gambol the crust
(snow frozen the night before)
as effortless angels, from wing to ski
gliding o'er the hills, undulant

The alpine vales' long, sweeping slopes –
all sweet-layered in flaking delicate:
God-heaven's primeval season.
By day, dazzling, at night
clear with stars surrounding
a bright transient moon.
Idealic, those days and nights
"flying the crust", as they say
on spring days such as these.

Canto Three: Upon the Snow
Robin: [having fun, despite danger]
Too engaged we are to feel
the danger perhaps we should.
Look at that sky beyond the hill:
such shades of loveliness, pink and purpling –
so fresh, so new this niveous expanse
These days of snow remade
for we alone, it seems.
Neko: [also soul-resurgent]
I have to say we find some pleasure too
even mid this banter
as heft-less as this powdered spray!
Robin: [unoffended]
We'll need no lamps tonight,
if the skies stay clear –
For the moon rises o'er eastern flanks
but an hour past "the westering sun."
Neko: And we're camping...where?

Robin: Far still, yet not so far we hope:
First down the western slope
turning east at Seventh Lake,
gain the ridge, we look for Lyra
(the patterned astral melody)
above western hills
then by the moonglade's light
we find our hidden camp, above an opening
astride the frozen creek.
Rough, and for years untended;
yet still well-supplied
mid rock and wind-bitten hemlock.
First we sleep, then after sundrop
ski up the frozen acclivity
toward the high pass – the only sure escape
from assassins Tartusian.
Neko: I'd rather be struck down on ski
beneath the hoary Titan fist
of these Arctic peaks
then fall 'neath the remorseless kiss
of Turkmen dart or steel –
Though neither fate is welcome!
Robin: "My heart does quiver and quail
beneath your brave charm."
Neko: [considering him as
they stride side by side]
I love that verse.
You've some merit, I grant:
the soft subtle flow

of limb as we weave the trees;
The bold intuitional spirit,
moving across the land you know and love...
Robin: And yet I'm nigh on brownshorting
thinking of those Arctic peaks.
Easily I move thru these lower hills
but the higher, steep slopes I've always feared.
Rashly, I've ventured there,
trying to surprise that fear
to return only more afraid.
(And quite tired and hungry.)
And yet there we must go...
Neko: Well, on to the camp for now, I suppose,
for a certain lady hath great need
overmuch just now of food and a warm place
to lay her weary bones.
Robin: We arrive in seven hours,
if we fly!
Neko: [as if to an invisible audience]
Seven hours?
And I was just coming to think him
trending toward the chivalrous!
[skiing off, the scene ends.]

Canto Four: Hidden Rocks
Neko: It's nice here, in the tent, so well secured.
Robin: Yes, amid the copse,
fringing this high alpine vale
of crumholtz and frozen tarn —

mid the rocks and deep-delved places
we plant this four-season moorage
able to shed the heavy drifts
off snow-shaded draping.
Neko: A foresight that could save our lives.
Perhaps not, but I sleep much more at ease!
And you brushed the tracks past Third Rock?
Robin: Yes, well brushed,
though still were possible...
Yet with the rising breeze, more brushed still –
We'll wake past sundrop
at full strength we hope. [long silence]
Robin: So, Shapur and Neko,
on the Illyrian Traverse?
Sounds epic: time with such as he,
in such a place.
Neko: He is impressive –
and safely married, of course!
Robin: Yes, and with child.
Yet at the time he was single...
but of that I'll not press.
How'd your tibia come to the splint?
Neko: A cornice failed
upon some steep declivity:
I fell, fortunate in God's small way
to land upon a ledge;
But it was rock, and my ski splintered
and bone snapped, hopelessly hobbling me.
I lay silent, so certainly alone –

yet not an hour later
Shapur happened by, his descent my equal
in skill, my master in fortune.
En passant, he saw me;
and climbed to regain my ledge.
He had rope... and strength –
after much pain and many hours,
we dropped into the trees
and more stable terrain.
On rough-fashioned sled
he dragged me until nightfall
only then admitting to having no food
and gently inquiring of my store.
Again *fortune favored the bold*
for I had extra, intending a further week
alone in the highland.
Four days later, we reached Silver Vale.
The break was clean – within six weeks I skied.
(Though it still ached a bit
during the fourth hours.)
So struck by his understated charm,
his over-chivalrous demeanor,
his soft humility...
Naturally, I maintained our acquaintance,
thus coming to party,
meeting you, and being pursued.
By the Tartusian killers, I mean.
Robin: Your story enriches me, truly
but my dear, shall we sleep?

Another night comes too soon.
Chorus: *Deep they sleep,*
in wide, sun-slanting surrender –
Bright visions flashing thru light-shorn dream
til the wee hours fade:
and Robin briefly wakes
to see the sun sink
beyond the far western hills –
and still on they sleep. [Hours pass...]
Robin: It's evening Neko, we must rise
for the sun-soft crust crispens
to accept our speeding strides
'neath moon-molten skies
the dwarf forest's half-cloaked slopes
and a gibbous waning just past full.
[They rise, dress and pack]
We've far to ski before the ice,
but we'll prevail, and make the train:
deeper in mountain, far from coast
where no agent of distant lands
would dream to seek.
Neko: They may find tracks
we've not covered
yet no greater plan can I now divine.
[while collapsing the tent]
This land of yours, the crag-close horizons,
the flaming mountains
framing such deep-bred care;
The valleys peopled, yet wild still

and the bonsail crumholtz, those twisting trees,
dwarven – for months under snow;
yet ennobled by millennia
beneath the tender parings of thy people –
And with the years, the trees take shape:
frosted nordic archers, still dripping
release from the great melt
of their hibernal tomb.
Robin: And in summer it's a land
grown even more glorious:
From glacier-nested cliff
down-cleaving mountain streams,
past where Alpine meadows cling
above shale cascades
(the finest rock skiing, they say,
west of Shambhala!);
A sky whose light never dies, a shade
issuing sweet vesperal cries
of purity and bliss;
A lingering twilight afore the dawn;
Aires alive in gentle suasion, hopeful whispers
half-spoken, yet felt and lived.
[done packing, they ski]
Neko: [seemingly unfazed
by his lumenist mysticism]
Rock skiing eh?
You know, out past the Crystalline Hills,
deep in the Revelations Range
along the steep slopes flanking Golgotha

in late spring, when the rock glaciers move most
one may ski down, quickening
(thru lunge and lope) in relative safety
even without leathers – so much fine-grain scree,
spills loose and easy down those peaks sublime!
[voice trailing] O, a host of other dangers
common to the sport, remain in play,
of course, and yet...
no evening blooms in deeper hue
than those fine, rock-ski days of June...

The End

Quotations
The portions quoted in this work are italicized.

Bound by Ancient Longing
Thou lovest, but ne'er knew *love's sad satiety*
– Shelley, *To a Skylark*
[Misquoted as *love's sad satieties*]

Glistering From Her Womb
Not in utter nakedness
But trailing *clouds of glory* do we come
– Wordsworth, *Ode: Intimations of Immortality from Recollections of Early Childhood*

Lost Tuvan Princess
She shone like a window of glass upon a far hill in *the westering sun*, or as a remote lake seen from a mountain: a crystal fallen in the lap of the land. – J.R.R. Tolkien, *The Lord of the Rings*

Pale Western Star
quote in classic raptures
– Lord Byron, *Childe Harold's Pilgrimage*

This ride was my delight. I love all waste
   And solitary places; where we taste
   The pleasure of believing what we see
   Is boundless, as we wish our souls to be;
– Shelley, *Julian & Maddalo*

*...to be wise and love
is hardly granted to gods above*
[possibly proverbial]

*Tis distance lends enchantment to the view,
and robes the mountain in its azure hue*
– Thomas Campbell, *Pleasures of Hope*

holy fire – Bruce Sterling, Title of Novel, 1997

Anywhere Out of the World
– Charles Baudelaire, Title of Poem

Shimmering Center
*none ever trembled and panted with bliss
In the garden, the field, or the wilderness*
– Shelley, *The Sensitive Plant*

*For my purpose holds, to sail
Beyond the sunset and the baths
 of all the western stars
 until I die.*
– Alfred, Lord Tennyson, *Ulysses*

When I behold, upon the night's starr'd face,
huge cloudy symbols of a high romance,
And think that I may never live to trace...
 – John Keats, *When I Have Fears That I May Cease To Be*

...The Last Page

Their breath is agitation, and their life
A storm whereon they ride, to sink at last,
And yet so nurs'd and bigotted to strife,
That should their days, surviving perils past,
Melt to calm twilight, they feel overcast
With sorrow and supineness, and so die...
– **Lord Byron**, *Childe Harold's Pilgrimage*

A loftier Argo cleaves the main,
Fraught with a later prize;
Another Orpheus sings again,
And loves, and weeps, and dies.
A new Ulysses leaves once more
Calypso for his native shore.
– **Percy Bysshe Shelley**, *Hellas*

About the Author
Robin Devoe is the *nom de plume* of Rob E. Earl – an Alaskan who enjoys word-collecting, poetry, skiing, cycling, and motorcycling. (Please dont judge him solely by this poetically pretentious photo – he's not *that* bad.)

Other works by Robin Devoe:
Dictionary of the Strange, Curious, and Lovely (2017, 2022); *Epic English Words:* Dictionary of Beauty, Interest, and Wonder (2022); and *Dictonary of the Rare, Creative, and Beautiful:* Words for Writers, Poets & Dreamers (2023).

Made in the USA
Middletown, DE
24 February 2024